Blessings,

Cathy

2012

Fields of Grace

Fields of Grace

everyday encounters with the Holy

poetry and photographs
for
reflection and meditation

Cathy Scherer Stubbs

Also by Cathy Scherer Stubbs:

Lullaby & Goodnight
An album of lullaby favorites from around the world
with soft vocals and gentle harmonies.
available on amazon.com, cdbaby.com, and other outlets

Fields of Grace is available at:
www.createspace.com/3691398, amazon.com
and other outlets

For comments and to view these photos in color:
fieldsofgrace.cathy@gmail.com

Photographs by Cathy Scherer Stubbs
Copyright © 2011 Cathy Scherer Stubbs
All rights reserved.
Printed in the U.S.A. by createspace.com
Library of Congress Control Number: 2011919331
Library of Congress Subject Heading: RELIGION/Inspirational
ISBN-13: 978-1466402201
ISBN-10: 1466402202

For my parents,

Wilfred (Hunk) & Beatrice Scherer

and grandparents,

Charlie & Lucy Scherer

who introduced me to the fields of grace.

CONTENTS

Attentiveness (cont.)

Lessons from Daily Life

Canticles

Alphabetical List of Poems

ACKNOWLEDGMENTS

This project would never have come to completion without the help of two people: Vic Klimoski, a fellow poet, who first suggested the idea and kept me focused; and my loving husband, Dan, my partner for the past 38 years, whose encouragement and support kept me going, and who spent countless hours scanning photos, and getting the final work ready for publication.

THANK YOU

Introduction

My relationship with the earth began even before I was born. On a warm day in late May, my father was helping a neighbor put up hay (unusually early that year), when he was told to get home right away, the baby was coming. I arrived later that evening, the second child in a family that would eventually include seven girls and three boys.

Surrounded by woods and fields, I grew up to the rhythm of the seasons, with the song of the red-winged blackbird playing in the background. Our farm had belonged to my grandparents, and we lived in the big farm house where my father was born. I didn't recognize the uniqueness of my life until I moved away – it was simply life on the farm.

Over the years I've kept journals with thoughts and insights often tied to nature. Photos I've taken were often starting points in my journaling. The photos range from the spectacular (blazing trees in autumn) to the mundane (a patch of dandelions). Like Anne Morrow Lindbergh, who came to see lessons in the sea and its offerings, I have come to see lessons in the world around me - lessons often captured in photos I've taken. Sometimes the message is loud and clear; other times it takes a while before the message surfaces. In the end, the poem may not take me where I expected to go, but it always leads me where I need to be.

When I write a poem from a photo, the first thing I must do is simply sit with the scene and let it fill me. I place myself in the photo, aware of the smells, sounds, and weather conditions. I start by describing what I see and feel; what my impressions are. If I find myself struggling for words, I know I am thinking too much, and have to back away, empty my thoughts, and begin again. Sooner or later I'm led to a new level of awareness where ordinary images unfold a larger Reality.

Once the basic poem is written, the next step is to make sure the ideas flow in the correct sequence without any gaps. I've also come to realize I'm never really finished with a poem. I find myself playing with sounds and rhythms of other words, always searching for the "perfect combination."

These poems reveal how ordinary images can give rise to new understanding, giving voice to something deep within. They reflect insights gained by being grounded in the present moment and open to the rich harvest contained in the fields of grace surrounding us.

"You will find something more in woods than in books.

Trees and stones will teach you that which

you can never learn from masters."

St. Bernard of Clairvaux

Marking
the
Seasons

Crocus

Just when I'd
  nearly given up,
  you break through.

Stunning
  testimony of
  Spring's return.

Forest Floor in Spring

Too impatient
  to wait
  for the others,
  they burst forth
  from below.

A solo voice
  echoing
  through the
  still-barren forest.

Daffodils

Deliberately placed,
  their appearance
  still a surprise.

Planted in hope
  they kept to
  themselves
  till now;
  journeying upward
  into the unknown.

Who could imagine
  the beauty
  hidden below?

Spring Field

Orderly lines
  fashion a pattern
  in newly-turned earth.

Seedlings in
  precise formation
  make way for the
  wisdom figure
  in their midst;
  acknowledging the
  presence of One
  greater than they.

Rainbow (no photo)

Passing through
  water droplets,
  sunlight scatters
  into colors;
  a streak
  of vibrant hues
  crossing
  once-threatening skies.

A promise of faithfulness.

Dandelions

Unwanted,
  unappreciated.

Appearing
  like clockwork
  each Spring.

Unfazed
  by criticism;
  emerging,
  celebrating
  returning.

Dandelions
  know how to live!

Symphony of Color

Like an artist using
  rich oils of sound,
  the leaves paint
  a symphony of color.

Vibrant reds,
  bright yellows,
  deep greens,
  each play their part
  to the fullest.

Melody,
  harmony
  and rich bass notes
  combine,
  presenting the season's
  brilliant finale.

Tree Branches in Autumn

Wrapped in black velvet,
 branches and trunks
 set off amber leaves,
 providing the
 framework for
 Autumn's spectacle.

Do I remember
 it is Love's
 faithful Presence
 that supports and
 gives life
 to my efforts?

The Golden Wood

Showers of sunlight
fall to earth,
dripping silently from
branches overhead,
forming a golden mist
on the forest floor.

Crumpled sheets of
yellowed parchment
gather in piles;
collecting like a poet's
unsuccessful attempt
to capture the moment.

Bare Trees

Surrendering to
  Nature's ultimatum,
  they've let go
  of past glory,
  preparing for
  winter's austerity.

Their nakedness
  offering a view
  beyond the immediate
  to a vista
  hidden in
  summer's high growth.

Cornfield in Winter

Hopes and dreams
   planted in
   another season
   languish in the cold.

Stoic mourners
   stand in
   respectful silence
   for a harvest denied.

Who would
   have thought
   winter would
   come so early?

Winter Sunset

Not for winter
  the raucous colors
  of other seasons:
  no blazing reds,
  oranges and yellows.

Cold, brittle
  days demand
  classic elegance.

Muted tones
  invite quiet
  contemplation,
  whispering of
  Love's subtle Presence.

Attentiveness

Log Bench

Come away
  to a quiet place;
  sit and rest.

Simply be
  at one with
  your surroundings.

Breathe deeply
  and celebrate the
  Presence
  in this moment.

Power Lines

Stoic guardians
of progress
pass in
single file,
power coursing
through their veins.

Heedless
of their surroundings,
they continue
uninterrupted;
disappearing from view
without a second glance.

Theirs is serious business.

Brick Buildings

Building blocks
of time,
given to all.

Some pile them
squarely upon each other
thankful to use them up,
relieved when they
don't fall down.

Others experiment
with shapes
and designs,
not satisfied to
simply use them up.

Herringbone stitches,
curves and arches,
circles and pointed gables
once seen as
impossibilities
take shape.

Graceful lines
soften straight edges,
surfaces take on
texture and ripples,
dimensions expand.

Completed structures
emerge,
reflecting
choices made.

Clothesline

Memories of heavy
  burdens made light,
  sweetened with the
  scent of sun and wind,
  hang in the air.

Drooping lines
  abandoned in favor
  of tumbled warmth
  wait patiently
  to be rediscovered.

Rusted poles with
  outstretched arms
  balance gracefully,
  frozen in time.

Shaded Bench

Shaded from the sun,
  a place of
  cool refreshment
  along the shore.

A gift
  for weary bodies
  and restless minds.

Cornfields & Woods

Disciplined fields
  bordered by
  unrestrained growth;

Their orderly rows
  wondering what
  freedom would be like.

Rope Swing

Suspended by a
silver thread
it invites me to play,
promising rest
from the business at hand.

Stepping toward it
in my mind,
I swing freely
before reluctantly
letting go.

The invitation remains
whether or not I accept;
a gentle movement
calling softly,
waiting.

Fenced Garden

Free from interruption,
  life bursts forth,
  coming to blossom
  without hesitation.

A place set apart,
  but not separate;
  allowing entrance
  to sun and rain.

The Garden is still here.

Frog Among the Flowers

Tucked away
   among the daisies,
   hidden from
   casual observers
   you sit quietly.

A moment of
   unlooked-for grace
   among the lilies
   for those with
   discerning eyes.

Picnic Table by the Shore

A sacrament of encounter
  offered each day;

Waiting to be received.

No dress code or
  reservations required.

Benches by the River

The trees have come
to take it in –
water for their thirst
and beauty
for their growth.

An invitation
extended to all:
"Stop,
rest awhile,
refresh yourself."

But we hurry by:
"Not today,
perhaps tomorrow."

The invitation
will be there tomorrow,
but the river of today
will be gone
forever.

Boot Planter

Thick soles,
  now abandoned,
  surrender quietly
  to journey's end.

Usefulness,
  once measured in miles,
  redefined;
  the future
  no longer certain.

Travel-weary stillness
  brings new insight;
  transformation
  brings new life.

Hay Bales in Winter

Graced moments
　　treasured and remembered,
　　providing nourishment
　　for leaner times.

Cemetery

Precise rows of monuments
  great and small
  stand in quiet witness
  to lives long-lived
  and unfulfilled tomorrows.

A place where
  completion and interruption
  lie side by side.

Where grief and sorrow
  find a measure of comfort
  in a sure and certain Design.

Stone Stairway

Arranged
with care,
worn smooth
by time;

Leading
to a place
only the trees
remember.

Cemetery in Winter

Lives valued
  and remembered;
  brief moments in time
  marked by stone.

A holy place
  of quiet reverence
  where fragile,
  sacred vessels
  are laid to rest.

Lessons
from
Daily Life

Frog Crossing

Sometimes it takes
 an official sign
 to slow us down,
 to see the life
 beneath our feet.

We're so busy
 looking up
 we forget
 to watch
 where we're going.

Moments of
 unexpected grace
 intersect
 our path every day.

Watch for the signs!

Pumpkin Hanging from Vine

Grounded fruit
look on in wonder:
"Not for me,"
"Too risky,"
"Unnatural."

The vine listens
only to the sun's call;
reaching up,
delighting in
new horizons
above the tall grass.

Patience, trust and
perseverance
support the vine
in its quest;
its fruit held fast by
sturdy ropes of faith.

Seeds of impossibility
are planted every day;
some see only an
impossible tomorrow,
others see a possible
TODAY.

Flowers Behind Fence

Planted safely
  behind the fence,
  they look in wonder
  at one of their own
  beyond the border –

As if overnight it
  decided to pull up stakes
  and strike out on its own,
  leaving safety and security
  in favor of adventure.

Daylily

I've never seen
  a shy daylily!

Each blossom
  greets the day
  enthusiastically;
  fully exposed
  to sun and rain.

Do I celebrate
  life each day;
  giving myself
  without reservation,
  willing to be
  vulnerable?

Milkweed

Opening wide,
  moving and
  expanding with
  every breath,
  tightly-packed potential
  explodes into
  endless possibilities.

There is no going back.

But who
  would choose
  cramped,
  dark quarters
  over this moment?

Wildflowers & Barbed Wire

Wildflowers
will not be fenced.

Sharp wire may
threaten others,
but not
the wildflowers -
growing under,
over and
through the barbs
without fear.

Beauty
has its way
in the end;
outlasting and
overwhelming
futile attempts
of control.

Rock Garden

Thick leaves
    double as petals,
    making the most of
    limited resources,
    wasting nothing.

Searching out
    pockets of soil,
    softening the landscape.

It knows what
    few would guess:
    even a rock can
    support life!

Trees from Rock

Seeds germinate
  between stones,
  setting down
  tenacious roots.

Anchored securely,
  they rise from
  solid rock;
  offering new perspectives.

Challenging assumptions.

Highway Memorial

Unfading blossoms
mark where
lives changed forever.

Passing motorists
spare a glance,
then hurry by,

Reminded suddenly
of their own
mortality.

Butterfly on Goldenrod

Balancing lightly
  on a single blossom,

Surrounded,
  but not overwhelmed
  by possibility;
  concerned only with
  what is before her.

Rejoicing in the moment.

Do I understand
  the lesson of the
  butterfly?

To recognize
  each moment
  as an opportunity
  to see and experience
  the Love before me.

I am called
  only
  to this moment
  in time;

To this life,
  this day,
  this place.

Canticles

Water Garden

Where does the rainbow
   go on a sunny day?

What songs play on the wind?

An invitation to stop
   and ponder such questions;
   imagining a song
   sung by the colors
   of the rainbow:
   solos on a sunny day,
   a grand chorus after the rain.

Moved by
   unseen rhythms
   I step out,
   dancing across the water,
   to the music of the rainbow.

Swing Set by the Sea

We all need help
  in the beginning –
  to be lifted up,
  given a push
  along the way.

We face the unfamiliar
  with a trusted
  presence nearby,
  our confidence growing.

Moving beyond
  necessary limits
  we step into the future.

Encouraged
  by the Love
  we have known,
  we make our way
  along shifting sands;
  life's possibilities
  echoing around us.

Marsh Marigolds

A life spent high
   above the forest floor
   offers itself
   to future generations,
   its task completed.

Its passing marked
   by golden voices
   raised in songs
   of praise and
   thanksgiving
   to the Author of Life.

Lilies of the Field

Roadside ditches
fill with
unexpected beauty
springing
from sand and gravel.

Bright colors topping
coarse stems
shout their song,
hoping to be heard
above the traffic.

Full Moon at Midnight (no photo)

Its silvery light
   creates a world
   unseen by day.

The silence is complete:
   even the colors have
   been turned off.

In this hushed moment
   there is no hurry,
   no sense of time's passing.

I hold my breath.

Deer on Hillside (no photo)

You stand before me
yet I do not see you.

A flicker of
movement
gives you away
before you blend into
the background again.

How many times
have You stood
before me
and I did not see?

Morning Mist Above the River (no photo)

Like souls of the just
  called forth from
  watery graves,
  ghostly shapes emerge,
  drawn to the Light.

Spiraling upward
  their forms disperse,
  then disappear from sight,
  enveloped completely
  in Love's warm embrace.

Water from a Stone Wall

Flowing from a gap
 in the stones,
 water appears
 from nowhere;
 a delightful surprise
 in a no-nonsense
 wall of rock.

How like
 Your Presence
 in my life.

A refreshing gift
 if I'm not intent on
 filling up the empty places.

Help me celebrate
 the gaps in my life,
 recognizing them
 as unique moments
 for encountering You.

Forest

Taking me
  by the hand,
  You lead me
  beyond the path,
  to a deeper
  Awareness.

Pointing out
  colors and textures;
  like an artist
  with a favorite canvas.

Oak Tree

Untrimmed,
 undisciplined;

Immense growth
 from a
 small seed.

Related,
 no doubt,
 to the
 parable tree.

Forest Path

Radiant sunlight
  filtering through leaves
  beckons me,
  providing a guide
  through the shadowed forest.

Enough light
  to find my way,
  but I yearn for more.

Love's warmth
  reaches me,
  holding forth the
  promise of a time
  and place without filters,
  where Love's intensity
  can be fully taken in.

Waterfall – Amazing Grace

Flowing over,
  overflowing,
  moments of
  overwhelming Love
  wash over me.

Unlooked for,
  unexpected,
  freely given,
  humbly accepted.

Ordinary elements
  carry a
  Divine message:
  "I am here....you are loved."

Alphabetical List of Poems

Made in the USA
Charleston, SC
04 April 2012